The Biggs: A Family Affair

Tell-All Account of America's Most Heinous Cannibals

Clyde Smith

The Biggs: A Family Affair © 2018

ALL RIGHTS RESERVED. NO PART OF THIS BOOK MAY BE REPRODUCED IN ANY FORM OR BY ANY ELECTRONIC OR MECHANICAL MEANS INCLUDING INFORMATION STORAGE OR RETRIEVAL SYSTEMS WITHOUT PERMISSION IN WRITING FROM THE AUTHOR, EXCEPT BY A REVIEWER WHO MAY QUOTE BRIEF PASSAGES IN A REVIEW. THE STORY, ALL NAMES, CHARACTERS, AND INCIDENTS PORTRAYED IN THIS WORK ARE FICTITIOUS EXCEPT FOR THE HISTORICAL FACTS, WHICH YOU SHOULD RESEARCH ANYWAY. NO IDENTIFICATION WITH ACTUAL PERSONS (LIVING OR DECEASED), PLACES, BUILDINGS, AND PRODUCTS IS INTENDED OR SHOULD BE INFERRED. NO ANIMALS WERE HARMED IN MAKING THIS WORK, ALTHOUGH MANY WERE MOST DEFINITELY HARMED ON THE BIGGS FAMILY FARM. MANY, MANY, MANY. PEOPLE ARE ANIMALS, AFTER ALL.

Table of Contents

Foreword 1

Chapter 1: Emigration 4

Chapter 2: Civil War and Reconstruction 12

Chapter 3: The World's Columbian Exposition 25

Chapter 4: Return to the Land 40

Chapter 5: High On the Hog 55

Chapter 6: The War Effort 71

Chapter 7: Too Big and Failed 82

Chapter 8: A Haunting Future 95

Foreword

Upon graduating from Georgetown Law in Washington, D.C., I imagined criminal defense as a moral obligation to my country. Even the worst of the worst were still human, and they still deserved competent defense. In all of my years as a defense attorney, for both rich and poor clients, clients of all backgrounds, my belief was never shaken. In my efforts, I was able to free dozens of wrongfully accused men through DNA testing, exposing purposely-mishandled evidence, and even exposing state corruption. I can say with pride that I was the man to see when wealthy elite stacked insurmountable odds against you.

When I graduated in 1973, I joined a small firm in Virginia called Shoemaker, Ballard & Drossman. As a new lawyer, I began assisting in the Biggs Family Case of 1965. Although I didn't know anything about it when I began work, I soon found that it was an ongoing investigation mired in colossal levels of burcaucracy, accusations so strikingly evil, they hardly seemed feasible and implications of corruption that

Tell-All Account of America's Most Heinous Cannibals

stretched all the way to the upper echelons of America's elite.

While continuing to handle my own casework, I began regular meetings with the Biggs Family at their patriarchal home in Chattanooga, Tennessee. It was during these meetings that the Biggs Family granted me access to their private archives dating back to their founder, Zebulon Leviathan Biggs, in 1859. Through their hospitality, I was allowed to stay in an unused cottage on the family farm where I could research their case.

Through my research and interviews of the Biggs Family, I soon became aware of the true horror lying within the Biggs walls, under their fields, and inside the stomachs of millions of unknowing Americans, both young and old, wrought by America's most odious family. I feel it is my duty to describe in these pages what everyone is afraid to read – that the Biggs Family is alive and well in nearly every community across this nation. Their roots run hellishly deep, and their twisted black branches, if made visible, could blot out the very sun.

The public must know what I have found. We must protect ourselves from the wraith- like tentacles of this old and evil family. But beware, dear reader, because what you are about to read is so shocking – so hideous – that it may change the way you think forever.

The Biggs: A Family Affair

"During a tour of the south, I happened upon an outfit called The Biggs Family Miracle Cures and Attractions; a snake-oil operation in Tennessee that travelled among county fairs selling gut-rot and garnering ticket sales through oddities and freaks. It was here I witnessed what appeared to be a giant cleaving another man asunder. There was no chance this was illusion! After the show, a different man came from behind a curtain claiming to be the cleft man. I approached the attraction owner to inquire on his trick. "No trick," he said with a tobacco-stained grin. I knew better. I warned the man that the law would surely catch up, if not sooner, than later. He laughed and said, "We'll charge 'em double!" It was this rare horror which convinced me that there's no such thing as bad publicity."

- P.T. Barnum, 1890

Chapter 1: Emigration

The first piece of evidence detailing the history of the Biggs family is a small well-worn scrap of paper, written in German, which denotes the sale of farmland to a Zebulon Leviathan, last name smudged. It is quite likely this land lie somewhere in eastern Prussia, but I can find no further corroborating evidence. Although he could have only been 21 years old at the time of sale, ZL seemed to have amassed quite a fortune. The date of the deed was 1857, and no additional information exists detailing how ZL came into this windfall, or what he did with his land afterward. One may speculate many things, but no evidence exists to this day.

However, by 1859, ZL Biggs began the first entries of a journal in which he bared his most intimate matters. The reader shall note I have taken the liberty to translate Zebulon's native German into modern English.

"It is with great hope in my breast that I arrive in New York a free man. Upon departing from my fatherland, over the European continent, and having been

berthed in the [smudged words] vessel Galathee, I begin anew in this New World."

Z L Biggs dated his entry March 2, 1859. Interestingly, in May 1859, the famous *New York Clipper* magazine ran an article detailing the April sinking of the great vessel Galathee.

"What misfortune God the creator hath wrought upon innocents through this act of divine intervention! Lost are the shipmate and captain who courageously rode out upon the Galathee as she returned mid-April to her European shores. Upon her departure, she carried no fewer than 150 passengers, 300 American slaves, various tradeable goods, and an assortment of American-made ivory and stone chess pieces, and their boards. All passenger and cargo logs, as well as those 150 precious lives, were lost in the deep blue maelstrom."

It is difficult to speculate whether or not ZL Biggs had any hand in the sinking of a passenger vessel such as the Galathee, but upon fully reviewing the history of this cruel family, dear reader, I assure you it is not outside of this evil man's powers.

The city of old New York was a rough and tumble town filled with avenue upon street, borough upon den of corruption, murder and malice. One would rightly assume this was the very environment intended for ZL Biggs to raise himself to a point of physical dominance. Many men of that era were known for their brutality and stark dealings in life and death. Yet, to know the patriarch of the Biggs is to know that the man had no stomach for one-on-one physical confrontations. Shadows were the atmosphere through which Biggs preferred to deal; silence, a rope around the throat, a blackjack to the skull; a knife piercing the organs of an enemy in some darkened alley amidst the noises of rattling rain overtop tin roofs. Perhaps it is strong to call Biggs a sneak thief, but one certainly would not compare him to William Poole of the Five Points in that era. In other words, ZL Biggs was no street tough, but instead, a calculating assassin.

Thus, it is of no surprise that a city like New York which was too wild, too populated, and which had too many journalists focusing on crimes of the day. Someone like ZL Biggs required silence, trust, and complicity. He gravitated toward this in the south.

In October of 1859, ZL Biggs purchased a transfer ticket through the Pennsylvania Railroad onto the Southern & Western Stagecoach Transfer Company for, "…safe passage to Chattanooga, Tennessee via Cincinnati, Ohio."

Dated April 23rd, 1860, a deed of sale reveals ZL Biggs purchased 40 acres of land for the stated purpose of farming. An unsent letter reveals Biggs' earnest excitement.

"I cannot fathom the simplicity in obtaining necessary funds by means of my own hands in order that I should purchase so much land in America. I plan to undertake an animal farm, raising chickens, goats and especially hogs. I have already purchased the necessary tools required for slaughtering, and I should think my neighbors would be appreciative if I should aide them during their October slaughters, as well. Now to the joyous art of husbandry!"

Biggs' ledgers reveal that acquiring a small herd of hogs, a dozen chickens, twenty sheep and a horse seemed to be no real problem. It would certainly imply that he had a source of money after reaching the states, and after purchasing his small tract of land. Obviously, in order to care for such animals, he would also have needed help in building the necessary means of containment, feeding, etc. While his ledgers reveal the cost of labor and materials, obviously no source is cited for the income.

Everything up to this point warrants further discussion, for there is no way to know specifically *who* ZL Biggs was prior to arriving in America. When pressed, the Biggs family maintains that ZL was a poor farmer from Eastern Europe with nothing more than tenacious will. But even a meager understanding of economics would suggest the man came from some means – or else how had he afforded the land in Prussia, the ticket to America, the trip to Chattanooga, the acreage, the animals and the implements to farm?

Aside from the pages you are reading, there has never been, and likely never will be, a full historical account of the Biggs family. Although what I am about to put forth is entirely speculation about ZL Biggs' heritage, I am so certain of its truth that I would stake my career and my life on it.

Frederick Wilhelm III, King of Prussia, had many children during his reign in the early 19th century. His youngest son, Prince Albert of Prussia, was known to have had a rocky relationship with his wife, Princess Marianne of the Netherlands. In fact, prior to his first marriage dissolving, and perhaps the catalyst for the dissolution, evidence suggests Albert had been having a passionate affair with the Princesses' maid of honor, Rosalie von Rauch. Rosalie and the Princess had been friends since childhood, so this cut the Princess deeply.

In 1836, Rosalie had a child out of wedlock whom she named Jakob Leviticus. She was forced to hide the boy from her family and her best friend, and thus, Jakob was passed to another noble family in Prussia who renamed him Zebulon Leviathan: Zebulon being the son of the biblical Jacob and Leviathan being the giant biblical sea monster. However, by the time Rosalie married Prince Albert in 1853, Albert's brother King Frederick William IV opposed the divorce and threatened to arrest the couple. Thus, ZL was forced to stay in hiding as before. Meanwhile, his father continued providing for him in any endeavor he chose.

ZL was likely encouraged to move to America for his own safety in 1857 so as not to appear a threat to the crown in a monarchy rife with assassination attempts and revolts. Unfortunately, immediately upon his arrival in America, he missed his uncle's stroke, and the resulting relaxation of the feud. By 1861, ZL's parents were allowed to return to the court of the King.

In any case, an unsent letter from ZL – one of so many – detailed his homesickness.

"Mother Rose, I miss you and father Albert with all of my heart and soul. I know that it is too late now for me to return, but I wish you to know that I am safe and happy here in America. It is a strange land, to be sure, but here every man is a king, and none need run from tyrants. I have for me a small land where I have built my home. To earn my keep, I will create a business in the land locally named Chattanooga, Tennessee, where I will raise animals. One day, I will return to you."

While ZL never again mentioned his parents by name, and while the rest of the Biggs family denies any ties to royalty, obvious similarities in naming habits through the family reflect their predecessors, including eventual heir Albert and first grandchild Waynelle Rose.

No additional records can be attributed to this point of Biggs' life. However, Biggs was prolific in his journal entries, as well as his letter writing. In fact, he wrote a number of letters, all unsent, detailing his own slow descent into depression, anxiety and, some might argue, madness.

In one letter, Biggs claims that the animals speak to him: "Their voices betray me often, saying, 'More milk, papa!' or, 'I'm cold, bring me to your bed.' Blast it, I haven't the time or fortitude for this treachery from them!"

Another letter details his strange affinity for butchery, "…and it is in this rupturing of the skin, and pouring out of life blood, that I feel most at ease. Here I am, covered, and I am most with God."

Chapter 2: Civil War and Reconstruction

In 1861, a nervous ZL Biggs, by now learning the English language quickly, wrote in his journal.

"I have received word this morning that I am to serve the Confederate States of America as an [sic] surgeon. I explained to the messenger that I had never once operated on another man, but had only the most rudimentary knowledge of veterinary medicine. Apparently, these military men have little concern for their countrymen, for I am packing my few tools and I am to report for duty tomorrow evening."

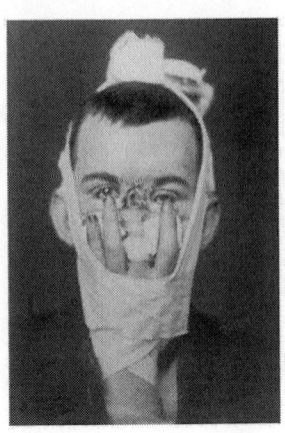

Like many immigrants in America, the reasons for fighting in the American Civil War were often no clearer than boundaries on a map. In fact, Biggs eschewed slave owning in his journal.

"Americans possess the strangest propensity for human subjugation that I have seen, even among the Dutch and English. While those Europeans have since abolished the practice, the Americans continue. What man should allow another man to plow his field, as if plowing his own wife, and to reap the joy of laboring for his own fruits? What man should fight to keep other men slaves, when he could be wealthy with much less effort? I hope I never understand some of the customs in this strange country."

While serving throughout Tennessee, Biggs began learning the surgeon's trade, or, as his journal details, "…how to enjoy taking apart men and putting them back together." Perhaps this fatal strain influenced Biggs' predilection for carnage. After all, many soldiers were no more than his playthings, already lamed up and soon to die. To Biggs, these powerless men were but open notebooks for experimentation. However, let it be known that Biggs was enabled by other surgeons nervous with his lack of skill. After all, why not teach the man how to practice on the soon-to-be-dead rather than bungling a surgery on a living patient?

During one particular series of surgeries on the battle wounded in 1862, Biggs was accused of "immoral experiments" involving the removal of organs "for show", the attaching of other patient's organs to the limbs and posteriors of others, as well as "...the wretched consumption of the insides of fallen soldiers."

The Connecticut based *Morning Journal and Courier* reported ZL Biggs' notoriety among both armies.

"...for he is called The Butcher of Missionary Ridge. Under his thirsty knife, soldiers and citizens from both sides of this terrible war are turned into feed for the horses. It is not from the cannonball or the musket round that the people of Tennessee should be saved, but from the calm hands and cool brow of this rebel doctor who portends righteous authority."

On November 26th, 1863, Biggs describes his harrowing escape from assassination by the advancing Union army near Lookout Mountain, only to be swiftly captured and interred into a prisoner of war camp. Given the conditions of those camps during that era, Biggs would likely have perished if not for a Sergeant Thomas McHenry who recognized Biggs as a surgeon from news accounts. McHenry, incorrectly believing Biggs to be of Scottish descent, provided the man extra rations and clean water. In later journal entries, Biggs mentioned the man.

"It is not my habit to linger over ugly matters in life, such as war, rebellion or the inequity of another man's soul. This habit of mine is held for moral reasons, but also in keeping my sanity. However, I sometimes falter when images of the War leak into my mind. I recall the men with whom I became dear friends. One man, however, was due my greatest thanks and respect, and yet, to him I could never return. His name was Sergeant Thomas McHenry, and while other soldiers in my company were left to starve, and ultimately die, Sergeant McHenry at least provided me the same rations he received, which included tobacco for a pipe, clean water, hard biscuits and salted pork. Compared to what I had been eating, it was excellent..."

Tell-All Account of America's Most Heinous Cannibals

Within two weeks, McHenry introduced the hack surgeon to none other than General Ulysses S. Grant. Biggs explained the event in his journal.

"...for I was to operate on the General at once. A musket ball had grazed the man's upper arm, taking some flesh with it, and although staunching the wound had successfully slowed his descent, the general was growing weak from loss. I simply sewed the wound shut with my hook and string — nothing else! The General, a man of jovial drink and story, fed me roast hen, game duck, braised beef, candied carrots, roasted potatoes, and such a varied assortment of liquors as to stupefy me into the morning. When we awoke quite cold and sick, he had me promoted into his army as a personal surgeon. My old threadbare gray uniform was taken, and provided to me were used blues from a fallen soldier. Thus, I begin my service in the Union Army!"

Unfortunately, within days of ZL Biggs' inception to the Union Army, Sergeant McHenry was shot. In a unique disclosure of sadness, Biggs wrote in his journal about the wound.

"I was unaware of who they would bring, but someone shouted that a man had been wounded on the battlefield and required immediate assistance. I removed my Union jacket and rolled up my sleeves, being sure to place the new garters the army provided me around my arms. My assistant prepared the tools just as they brought the man in and threw him on the table. My God in Heaven it was Sergeant McHenry.

His chest was rising with breath, but a hole in its side revealed bubbling and bleeding. We compressed the wound with bandages to try to stop the bleeding, and as we did so, we could hear the slightest sucking sound. The Sergeant had come in groaning, but not he was almost unconscious, turning white and his breathing was growing shallower. I called for the other doctor, but he did not arrive. I stood helplessly holding the wound and waiting for no one. The Sergeant died.

Time waits for no one, and it seems that just as soon as you are placed on this earth, you die and are forgotten. Thomas McHenry, the man who had helped me live, looked into my eyes and a whisper passed his lips — the whisper of his life among the cacophony of the world, gone all at once to never return."

Within the first few months after the end of the War, Biggs remained relatively reclusive. He haunted various forts waiting for his orders to return home. As soon as he received them, he left without much ceremony.

Biggs received a summons to Washington, D.C. where he was awarded the Medal of Honor for his service in the field. While he certainly had experienced some loss, there was no mention in any newspaper accounts for his butchery of fellow human beings, or his wanton and bizarre experimentation.

However, one photo exists deep within the archives, of which I have witnessed, revealing his shameful and sick practice on another. The photo is simply too gruesome to view, and is kept under lock and key within the Library of Congress. But rest assured, it is the vilest thing one could lay eyes upon. An arm, twisted and broken, was sewn onto a man's back, then enters the chest cavity on one side only to exit through the other where the remaining flesh is sewn on. It is as if the arm penetrates the same body from which it originates. And that is only the portion I am willing to describe, for the eyes are much worse.

In 1866, ZL Biggs filed for, and received, a US patent detailing several specialized medical instruments for performing dissections and amputating limbs. Although the instruments appear to be unequivocal in their intended use, likely acting as forbearers of future tools of their kind, one can only wonder how it was that an immigrant farmer with no medical background became so adept at his art.

Among the various patents, ZL Biggs created three unique cutting tools including the "protracted scalpel", the "ovoid boning blade", and the odd "box scissor". One could speculate at length on the similarity these tools share with crude butchering implements. However, it is a fact that the tools became quite popular among anatomists and medical professors. Although the resurgence of human dissection was still considered ghoulish, partly due to the propensity for body snatching and grave robbing, many respectable doctors continued the practice.

A cautious 1867 article printed in *The Boston Post* detail Biggs' moderate success, thanks in part to his connections with US Grant.

"...among the cadavers in the theatre, the personal surgeon to US Grant, George F. Shrady, demonstrates his knowledge of human anatomy at a dissection in the Ether Dome. Many such presentations are available to students of medicine, as well as the tenebrous 'night show' involving certain elements of the public. Shrady posits, "Such demonstrations would be nigh impossible if not for the recent inventions of Z. Levi Biggs, a surgeon in the Union Army..."

Early the next year, after Biggs had returned to his farm in Tennessee, settling back into a life of quiet husbandry, newspaper reading and general boredom, Ulysses Grant sent an ambiguous letter to the prosperous bachelor Biggs dated January 15, 1868, explaining a situation that, by most accounts, would have seemed commonplace if not for the strangely pleading tone.

"...so you understand, Emma's husband J. Salmon was cut down at Antietam within moments of Lee's retreat. Because that skunk McClellan refused to give chase, Sal's sacrifice was much in vain. The tale so roused our men that a sergeant dared to present it to that slipshod goose Lincoln, and he sent McClellan back to New York. But surely you appreciate that no show of force would right Emma's broken heart...

"...and thus, she remains without a husband in an era rife with coarse behavior and devil's promises. Although the parlance of our cruel time should insist that sweet Emma shall always be a bitter widow, a luckless spinster living with our family until she goes mad, I can attest sincerely that she is a peach ripe for picking. Her handsome features cause men to tarry; her porcelain skin appears angelic in any light. A shame that she is lost to time. A shame that she has no husband."

There is little doubt Grant was successful in swaying Biggs. A certificate of marriage from the Presbyterian Church in Chattanooga dated April 1, 1868, brought together in holy matrimony a Zebulon Leviathan Biggs aged 32, and Emily Marbury Dent aged 32. This union proved to be pivotal in Biggs' life as this not only cemented his connection to America's elite, but it formed the basis for a lifetime of unconventional partnership.

Shortly after the wedding, Emma Biggs begins a new diary.

"...and within the month, we move closer to my family in New York. My new and most wonderful husband Levi has put my fears to rest! We shall keep the family farm in Tennessee under the care of his younger brothers Johan, who likes to be called James, Lamprecht, who we call Larry, Jorg, who prefers George, Justus, who we call Jerry, and Hartmut, who we call Harry. Such a wonderful family of which I am now a part."

Ironically, whereas Biggs could not start in New York as an urchin or a beggar, he now willingly returned a man of great means, lurking, both literally and figuratively, in the shadows of society, with the implements to commit his crimes as well as to hide from them. While Biggs was most pleased to maintain a solidly middle class home with only two servants and a carriage, he very well could have afforded much more, if not for his own position of power within the American aristocracy, then at least by his own financial fortune. Yet, that was not the man, Biggs. He preferred the solitude and anonymity. And silence.

Although US Grant was accused of corruption and nepotism on many occasions, some unfounded and others notorious, reasonable evidence exists that leads us to conclude he had also offered a branch to Biggs in order to care for Grant's sister-in-law, and Biggs' new wife, Emma.

In a letter dated June 14, 1870, US Grant gives notice to Biggs that he will be hiring the so-called surgeon as part of his own personal staff.

"...naturally, I don't expect you to travel to Washington every time I come down with the cold, but I will request your presence during matters of state. To this, I am of course referring to our Grand Lodge. You will assume position under George [Shrady] as a White House family doctor and your wage shall be $3900 a year or $75 weekly. I believe this handsome sum should more than adequately care for our Emmy."

Thus, the mold was cast. His involvement in Grant's scandals remained hidden through the end of Grant's presidency in 1877.

A wealthy man, Biggs had amassed a fortune through his own federal position, his successful farming business and through sale of his patented medical equipment. The Biggs' now partook in urban life, sometimes sending money back to the family farm at the request of his younger brothers. Although to this point, his only crimes seemed to have been the sick and twisted experiments he'd performed during the War, Biggs was also making a fortune elsewhere. Only one diary entry alludes to, what appears to be, a business of body snatching.

"Jeremiah insists on young ones, to what purpose I cannot ascertain. Natheless, Kline and I often ply them

with candy and tickle them for sport. Like my little hogs at the farm, we love them and pet them profusely, bringing them to Jeremiah's laboratory in the evening and laying them to rest. The Black Boot in the Bronx serves a glass of beer for three cents and a hot supper with bread for two cents. With these little piggies we brought to market, Kline and I were fine and drunk this evening."

Daily newspapers rarely comment on the routine activities of street urchins, no matter their age. However, after a rash of disappearances, and grisly reappearances, the *New York Star* thought it prudent to mention, "…Mothers, beware your children. For whatever lawless forces act upon the streets of this city, they are sometimes want to remove the heads from errant boys."

Chapter 3: The World's Columbian Exposition

Much has already been said about the Chicago World's Fair of 1893, but none so eloquently as *The Devil in the White City* by Erik Larson. In discussing this chapter with him, the author admitted some of his frustration during his writing.

"...I'd always wondered about this elusive Biggs character. I mean, he was kind of a Punxsutawney Phil: he'd poke his head out and then scurry back into his cave. I would love to have included him in my book, if only I could prove any of it. Unfortunately, there were no reliable primary sources describing him; only anecdote, rumor and whispers."

Erik Larson was correct; if not for the Biggs family archives, there would be scarcely any sources tying Biggs to the Chicago World's Fair of 1893. Perhaps this is rightly so, for the fair was momentous for many things good and worthy of attention. In other words, as much a villain as Biggs may have been, including his famous cohort soon to be noted, the event itself was much larger and more important than the man. At most, he was just another actor involved in making the Fair so interesting.

Stepping back nearly ten years before the Fair was even conceived, ZL Biggs happened on a chance meeting that would change his life forever and begin the branches of the family tree. His journal explains the exchange.

"...I was introduced to a curious man named Dr. Herman Mudgett. George [Shrady] had become acquainted earlier during the young man's studies at the University of Michigan while producing a work on human anatomy with W. James Herdman. Evidently, this Mudgett was quite interested in slicing open the bodies of young women, to which both Shrady and Herdman apparently felt quite uncomfortable. In any case, they overlooked his bizarre interest as he showed such great zeal in acquiring cadavers in order that the three men could practice."

While neither man exchanged correspondence after the meeting, and where Biggs did not expound upon the interaction beyond his original entry, two years later, Biggs writes about Mudgett in glowing terms. This, even after the revelation that Emma and ZL became estranged.

"...she's grown distant of these last fifteen years. She does not bear children, an affliction that is a fault of nature and has driven her to desperation. Although I

cannot confirm it, I suspect she has had a number of gentleman callers while I am away in her attempt to become pregnant. I cannot fault her. I do love her, God knows...

"She will remain in New York with her family. I have seen that she shall receive a monthly stipend. We shall not ruin her name by applying for divorce, but I have given her permission to live freely once more. I believe her family has arranged to 'marry' her off to someone else, or else send her into an asylum. She's already taken on the additional surname Casey, which is evidently some invention of her sister's. I can only wish her luck.

"...meanwhil e, I look forward to greeting Dr. Mudgett upon my arrival in Chicago. He tells me that he's quite prosperous there, having opened a pharmacy. He is already in partnership with a number of investors

and plans to erect a building from which he will continue to ply his trade."

Biggs ceased writing in his journal during his transition from New York to Chicago, but he resumed writing during the early spring of 1888, when he explains that Mudgett, to whom he now refers as H.H. Holmes, has shown interest in a full set of Biggs' tools.

"It is unfortunate, though, that he cannot pay for these items, and they are not inexpensive. However, I believe he will find a means of producing the necessary funds in order to have them because he shows such great interest."

To Biggs' surprise, a letter from Chattanooga arrived in the mail on July 6, 1888 from his brother James.

"I know it would pain you, brother, to loose [sic] the farm under such stress as you been having, but the familys [sic] been growing considerable, and business has not been real well. Also, probably worth mentioning everyone is getting the bug around here. So while you are away, we plans [sic] to strike out on the off-season and make a little extra money. We are following county fairs around Tennessee under the name of The Biggs Family Miracle Cures and Attractions, *and we hope to make enough to set things right. Send any money you can. Meantime, love from everyone."*

The Biggs: A Family Affair

While entries are sparse in Biggs' journal during this period, many portend that he and Holmes had founded a lucrative relationship. Biggs often notes his travels to medical colleges, having secured cadavers from Holmes, eventually exchanging a full set of Biggs' instruments for Holmes use. While at these colleges, Biggs demonstrates not only his tools, but explains his specialized methods of flaying the dead so that the skin can be kept for "other purposes".

No records, public or private, verify his trips to these colleges, but sales receipts from anatomical schools, funeral homes and universities are clear that he became a rich man on these fruits alone.

While there is little information on Holmes' source of cadavers, it would seem Biggs was giddy about his assistance in procuring fresh bodies. In the early winter months of 1889, Biggs writes excitedly in his journal.

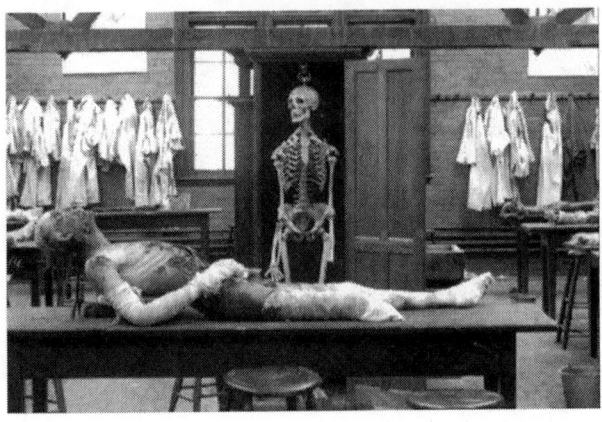

"We have already found three women to work as clerks in Holmes' pharmacy, each one more precious than the next. Although I am an older man now, I find my vitality marches through my veins stronger than ever before. Certainly, these women carry on like bleating lambs at the slaughter, but I believe this noise, the awakening of their souls, excites me the most."

Meanwhile, Biggs ties to the eastern United States wealthy had not been forgotten. Although he had been dropped from most invitations to stately events, his gracious handling of Emma's estrangement earned him a continued respect among the elite. While he was working with Holmes in procuring cadavers, and performing unspeakable things to them while they still lived, Biggs received a handwritten invitation requesting his presence at the 1892 Bohemian Grove Spring Jinks. The motto on the card read, "Weaving Spiders Come Not Here."

Even as a semi-married man, stories of ZL Biggs' chicanery at the Spring Jinks were legendary among wealthy men from New York to Boston and from Portland to Charleston. A wealthy socialite named A.J. Jeffries wrote in a letter to a business partner, "…and with that, the naked Levi Biggs set off into the woods atop a young maiden, slapping her backside with a riding crop and bucking her as if she was a strong colt!" Other writers allude to much more egregious inequities, but never identify the act, typically only referring to Biggs as, "that old Satan at his work again," or claiming things like, "the ghoul has trapped another, by god."

However, it is upon returning to Chicago that the story twists. Although quite open in his exploits with

H.H. Holmes, it would seem that Biggs was hiding a salacious secret from his partner.

"It appears Holmes' wife, Myrta, has become pregnant quite by mistake. And to think, I had partially lay blame for Emma's barren womb upon myself! In order that Myrta not suffer the same fate as Holmes' clerks, I have decided to send her to the farm so that she can bear the child and be protected among family. She has strict instructions to leave at once on a Pullman headed east. I shall recover her when this matter with Holmes is resolved."

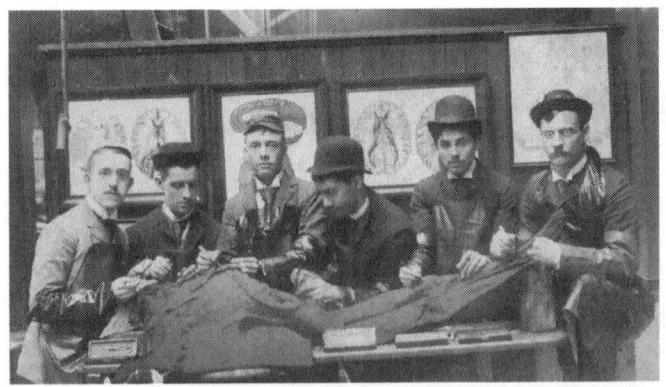

Although no official record exists, a single photo survives of the two babies, fraternal twins, named Judith and Zeb born in late 1892. The photo does not include the name of the photographer, but the odds were that Biggs paid for a studio session in order that Myrta would have something nice to send her family.

The Biggs: A Family Affair

Late in 1892, after much preparation, a notarized bill granted Z. Levi Biggs permission to set up an exhibition near the Midway Plaisance at the World's Columbian Exposition. His exhibition was erected in the Zoopraxographical Hall where Biggs showed his *Theatre of the Puppet*, a lurid display of flayed cadavers hung by thin chains and wires, posed in various grotesque fashions such as two dancers, a baseball player, a man holding a rifle with a flayed dog at his side, and many others. In fact, throughout the entire year of the Fair, Biggs' cadavers changed to serve his whimsy. The Chicago Tribune described it best in early 1893.

"We insist that the only fiend who could find such iniquitous filth entertaining as is displayed at this World's Fair's exhibit, the so called Theatre of the Puppet, would be the very Devil himself. Within the Zoopraxographical Hall wherein the exhibit resides, there hangs such ghastly smells that hordes of flies and their worms congregate near the horrific carnage strung up for display like a common butchers. If not for the bizarre poses forced upon the dead, this macabre display would offend even the rudest thug."

As an interesting side note, Biggs continued receiving invitations, every year until his death, to the shadowy Bohemian Grove Spring Jinks held in June. This was the only time in 1893 that Biggs writes, "I left the exhibit in care of Wilson, who, although young, is adept in the medical profession, and so understands the necessity of our work." Wilson is never discussed prior to, or after, the Exposition, and Biggs also does not discuss his trip to San Francisco.

Although the Biggs family did not keep ledgers from the World's Fair, Biggs does not parse words in his journal as to the success of his undertaking.

"Quite frankly, I've become rich by sales alone, as well as through contracted offers to perform at surgical theaters across the country. My previous wealth pales in comparison to this new fortune, and I am want to find means of spending this excess!"

The Biggs: A Family Affair

After the World's Fair, the wealthy Biggs continues living in Chicago, experiencing fine dining, exquisite entertainment and murder. A number of entries allude to his and Holmes' love for chasing down young women, only to clean their corpses and sell the bones. Biggs doesn't seem to mind that he was ruining lives.

"I do not consider myself a thief, yet on the other hand, one cannot help but sneaking a view through the personal effects of a wayward young woman. Inside a particular maiden's belongings, I found and unsent letter to a certain Mrs. Gerald Hammersmith, the girl's mother. She remarked on her excitement to afford tickets to the World's Fair after working in a shirtwaist factory for nearly one year. I think to myself what it must be like to be both poor and dead. It must be frightful.

For nearly a year, the pair of murderers trapped and killed dozens, if not hundreds, of unsuspecting young women. However, the tides were about to change as the hideous H.H. Holmes was forced to go out on the lam in his escape from police. After the murder of his friend Ben Pitezel, Holmes murdered the deceased man's children and kidnapped his wife, headed for Canada. Finally, upon being apprehended by the Pinkertons in Boston, Holmes was to be brought to trial for his crimes.

Biggs makes no mention of this apprehension, and in fact, describes the subsequent trial in October 1895 as, "…a fruitless display of smoke and mirrors." For, as it was told by Biggs, Holmes had never been captured, but remained in hiding at Biggs' Chicago residence.

"Perhaps I should feel some sense of remorse for the poor pinhead they placed on trial in Herman's place. The man's lawyer has already sworn under oath that this cannot be Holmes, and would recognize the doctor clearly. The judge laughed it off.

"Unfortunately for that poor soul, when they hang him, they will not be hanging H.H. Holmes, but a decoy put in his place by men of great power and wealth. However, Holmes will be judged all the same, at the least, on account of Myrta. I will see to that myself."

In November 1895, while Holmes was supposed to be sitting in a courtroom on trial for the murder of Ben

Pitezel, and after supposedly having confessed to 27 murders, Biggs wrote of his delectable dinner with Holmes in an upscale Chicago restaurant.

"...in which we dined upon large beef steaks, cooked rare with blood still cool at the center. For our next course, we enjoyed salmon smoked and on the bone, followed by duck soup with the little animal's feet and snout as garnishments... And after we thought we could eat no more, we forced upon ourselves a cheese cake, a cup of strong dark coffee and raspberry sherbet."

What follows is a strange and murky account that has unfortunately little other evidence to assist in shedding light on the final days of the murderer H.H. Holmes. *The Chicago Inter-Ocean Newspaper* described the fate of Holmes' "Murder Castle".

"Late in the evening on Sunday, witnesses claim two men entered the Castle with bags slung across their shoulders. One witness, Elba Maurice of Englewood, claimed that one of the men was in fact H.H. Holmes, the murderer currently on trial. Another witness claimed that the second man was a known cohort of Holmes, but no name could be ascertained... After spending only five minutes within the Castle, witnesses say the two men left at a quick pace and disappeared shortly before two large blasts rocked the structure, bringing it toppling down on itself and setting fire to the ruins... Police say special tools, which were to be taken as evidence, had remained

in the structure's basement at the time of the blast, but could not be retrieved."

A brief letter to Myrta is the only clue noting the whereabouts of the infamous Dr. H.H. Holmes.

"I return to you in Tennessee in five days' time. Please ask the family to prepare for my return and we shall all have a grand meal when I arrive. I shall be positively famished from this trip!

Please also put your sweet heart to rest, for he is dead. He shall harm you no longer. And they will never find him. The students at the University of Michigan will see to that."

On March 29, 1896, the *Chattanooga Times* wrote an article hailing the return of their prodigal son.

"... thus returns the courageous war surgeon Z.L. Biggs, bringing with him his fortunes made at the Chicago World's Fair Columbian Exposition, which recently closed in October 1893. Although Mr. Biggs is the purveyor of medical instruments, as well as a favored lecturer among medical schools across the nation, he has chosen to resume work on the Biggs' family farm, producing livestock for rendering."

Without much notice or fanfare, and within little under a year, families began reporting disappearances of young Tennessee boys and girls, some as young as five and six years. Meanwhile, men and women, often looking for work, were said to have disappeared in their efforts to find jobs locally.

It is simple to only blame ZL Biggs for his hellish lust for murder, but let us not forget the rest of the family, for whom murder was no issue. Biggs writes about his brothers taking so- called wives from these victims.

"I don't necessarily approve of their jovial little game, but what harm is it when the women end up expiring nonetheless. So I afford them their last insults upon these young things prior to their butchering. After all, the boys need to blow off extra steam after long hours at work, even if it means offending the meat before evisceration."

Chapter 4: Return to the Land

The century was nearing its turn and ZL Biggs, now 60, had witnessed many changes to the once-wild country he'd known for thirty-seven years. Yet, rather than simply retire back to the family farm, retreating to the anonymity of a relatively small livestock operation, Biggs set out to open one of the largest hog farming operations in the world.

"Biggs Meat Shoppe" Chattanooga, TN

Up until this point, ZL Biggs' family had not necessarily been apt livestock farmers. During their best year, they raised just enough to feed their ever-increasing kin with very little to bring to market. Some years, the family had to find other meat. Once ZL returned, records show he managed to raise 200 head of fattened hogs for slaughter in as little as four months. This is no extraordinary feat until one considers that Biggs did this single-handedly, only after having fed the family for a year, and after already having managed to repair or replace what lay fallow or ruined.

An October 31, 1896 bill of sale shows Biggs paid for transport of his hogs from the *Nashville, Chattanooga & St. Louis Railway*, onto the *Gulf, Mobile & Ohio*, and finally to the Union Stock Yard & Transit Company in Chicago, colloquially known as The Chicago Stockyards.

There is nothing to indicate the transaction somehow went poorly, or that Biggs received an unfair price. Later journal entries reveal otherwise.

"Those fools think they can charge me to simply hand over my livestock for killing? By God, I could have done it all myself had I known their phony rig! My brothers may lack motivation but money will remediate them."

Interestingly, ZL Biggs' journal appears to have abruptly halted February 7, 1897 when, upon inspection, I found 38 pages neatly sliced from the binding. Why had these pages been removed? Perhaps the patriarch was hiding something from the world. Or perhaps he was hiding it from kin.

The journal resumes on March 21, 1897 with grim news.

"...my little piggy, Myrta, needed something new. Myrta dear, there were so many things I had yet to understand about the way you worked inside. What was I to do when you sent all the sheep chasing away? Ten, and one, and one hundred. Twelve and Eleven. It is all the same to me, and now it is the same to you. Perhaps you will rest now and cease all of that mournful screaming. I shall miss you, dear. From ashes, to ashes, from dust to dust."

Within days of the entry, Biggs received a letter from his estranged wife, Emma. While it appeared to be the harmless conversation between former lovers, it ended strangely for a man who had just lost his second wife.

"...we all plan to see you soon, Levi. Perhaps you might steal away early and spend time with me? But I shan't count upon it. You will return and we will burn the remains. Let my transgressions, and your thirsty passions, rekindle this immortal fire. Free me from my genies' bottle."

As was his habit, "that old Satan" ZL Biggs attended the yearly Spring Jinks at the Bohemian Grove. In his absence, his brothers took charge of a now colossal 1,000 hogs at the farm, one of them sending a postcard to kin in Ohio.

"Brother Levi is out in calyfornya [sic] and done left us with a heap of pigs. He told me to tell ya'll to come on out to the farm as soon as you are able seein as we need all the help we can get for operations coming up. He ain't put up what he has in mind, but I guess we expanding right big soon. And we are killing soon to [sic]."

In July of 1897, ZL Biggs returned to Tennessee with his bride, Emma Biggs. The aging woman was described by Biggs as, "...wearing not but a bed linen strapped around the waist, uncut and flowing; some apparition, ethereal and intoxicating, floating onto the farm in stone silence, with God's steel in her blue eyes."

I found a single clipping from the *Buffalo Morning Express* in the Biggs Archive. Although it would appear to have no relevance to the Biggs family, it was neatly folded within ZL Biggs journal on the page describing Emma's return to the farm. The article details the escape of a certain "Miss Jane" thought to have been "dumped" on the premises by wealthy family.

"...we wonder how such a woman, deemed so criminally incompetent as to risk liability among the general public, could find her way out from the west wing of the Buffalo State Asylum without being spotted, and with no hindrance from staff. Superintendent Doctor Thomas S. Kirkbride claims the woman was under strict lock and key, and yet the police search the streets of Buffalo even now...

...Although Doctor Kirkbride claims the woman is often harmless, he warns that she is of old Irish descent, and so may become savage unexpectedly... If you are in the surrounding neighborhoods of Buffalo, beware a ghostly woman at your door!"

So striking was her countenance, James Biggs couldn't help but mention her in a letter sent to relatives west.

"...she is an apparition at least, and a Satanic wraith at worst. Her presence alone brings a chill to a room until you go find a coat. Her eyes, always watching, are like death's hand pointing at you... she celebrates silently, the death of anything and everything. Her eyes light up and widen as big as saucers when we kill for dinner. Even the cussed animals are scared stupid. Her gaze is intolerable, and she sits for hours staring through you."

In an acrid journal entry, ZL Biggs grouses about Emma's treatment.

"...I have told them the very last time, all of those jackals: Emma will stay here until she lies rotten and stinking in the earth. Certainly, she is odd among us! I

should know best. She does not take supper with the family, but eats in her room alone. She spends hours stirring about the cellar calling out to the spiders. I even provided her a kitten for some kind of comfort, and she immediately abused it until death, eating it raw with her bare hands, fur and claws and all. But it is not her violence that upsets them, it is her refusal to abide company. Can you imagine? These imbeciles have no opinion on her strange behaviors, but don't find her as agreeably drunk as they are?"

After her return to Biggs, Emma did not write in a journal or send correspondence for the remainder of her life except one odd letter. In it, she puts forth a strange request to her family, the Dents, in a seemingly uncharacteristic manner.

"…I am happy here with my family, and I ask that none of you pursue me. It is with great pleasure that Levi dotes upon my every need, feeding me, bathing me, and letting me walk out alone in the sunshine. I have even begun to love his children, Judith and Zeb, and I act as their mother after the poor woman passed away…

"If you could find it in your hearts, please send money so that our poor family can restart our farming business. We will take anything at all. It has been hard times since Levi returned to this dirt farm without anything but his aging hands and a broken back. But we shan't trouble you anymore. Please find it in your hearts to come through for us. We wait in anticipation of your next letter."

For the next three years, in between bouts of depression and madness, ZL Biggs confesses that work is difficult and he receives little help running the business. However, he finds it reassuring that his brothers are at least willing to handle the hogs, something ZL simply cannot do at his age. Although Biggs discusses very little pertaining to events outside of his business during this time, the rumblings of something big are brought to the forefront in an advertisement run through the Chattanooga Times, March 16, 1900.

"MEN WANTED for long hours, hazardous work with animals and machinery, raising and slaughtering livestock. Any color accepted. No experience necessary,

butchers preferred. Wages after first three months. Room and board provided. Call Biggs Farm, Chattanooga, Tennessee, Z. Levi Biggs."

Not much time had passed since the twins' birth, but in late May of 1900, they began a "twin journal", passed back and forth between the two to share their most intimate secrets.

"I write with such a sadness in me. Zeb and I both miss mamma awful. She is there in our hearts, and sometimes in our dreams. One night we heard her scream. Papa came in the room shortly afterward and put us back to sleep. He said she'd had a night terror. But then we never saw her again…"

Shortly after Judith's first entry, Zeb affirmed what the two knew deeply in their hearts.

"I'm tired of that witch, Emmy. She ain't my mom, and she ain't my stepmom. Uncle Larry says pop's story about mama goin on a boat to England is bunk. She was killed and fed up to the pigs. I bet it was that lunatic troll who done it. To Hell with her… And if I lay eyes on that damn Emmy sneaking around in our room again eatin flies, I will woop [sic] her, you bet."

The Biggs: A Family Affair

Hatred of Emma seemed to subside, or at least fall dormant, over the next thirteen years in the family. The twins' journal often refers to her as, "...that damned witch," in passing commentary on Emma's typical bizarre behavior, but little else is said. If many letters were sent out, few were received. Other irrelevant news clippings are in abundance, but not worth detailing, as they hold no significance to Biggs history.

However, even during this dormancy, entry after entry in ZL Biggs' journals revolve around his obsessive bookkeeping, strange voices he hears in the night, and paranoid delusions about his brothers. Here, as the aging patriarch reaches 77, we begin to see him for what he is; a lonely madman kept in isolation, more interested in work than life.

"Some have called me a sorcerer because I can turn lead into gold. I argue they are fools. For what use is gold if you lie starving and weak? If I be a sorcerer, it is because I can turn life into life, energy into energy; I change the bounty of earth into blood, and I consume it whole.

...If he requires a sacrifice, I obey. For what am I but a vessel?"

Meanwhile, in peculiar anonymity among insane family, the twins began growing and changing. It is difficult, at this point, to dislike them as their journal merely points to two children going through difficult growing pains, as well as emotional trauma through the loss of their mother. Unfortunately, they are often kept at the farm and not allowed to leave. They sometimes complained about feeling cooped up on the property, but otherwise, no mention is ever made of their leaving.

Thus, having grown quite intimate through their years in relative isolation, the siblings did what any young couple would do in their situation.

"Maybe we ain't as moral as mama. Maybe we ain't as smart as papa. But we love each other, and no one can take that from us. We have a bond that's closer than anything on this farm. I love Zeb and I know he loves me. We sometimes used to sit out on the lake and look up at the stars, and Zeb would say we should be together forever. So we ran out to the parson and got married."

While the marriage of fraternal siblings is shocking of its own, what followed that year was enough to stun the whole Biggs family. Zeb writes about the new expectations held over him.

"…well even papa seems cross with us, although he ain't said nothin. He told me I better get my life straight and start thinking about the family business, or else how was I gonna make up for this. Says a man's gotta work hard for his family. And now that we got a new one coming, I needed to take care of my sister better than ever."

Judith writes a different entry, explaining, in more tender detail, her obligation.

"When I took Zeb as my husband, I knew we was going to have children of our own someday. I guess the family just wasn't ready for me to start showing the little bump on my stomach. They all thought I'd snuck into town and got messed up with some man, but I straightened them out and told them about Zeb. Papa kissed me and said I was still always going to be his little

piglet, so my heart was saved. Now all I got to do is wait for the baby. When it comes, we'll love it just like mama loved us."

Nine months later, as 1913 closed on the family farm, now a massive hog operation reeking of acrid waste, stinking fires and sour mud, ZL Biggs and his brothers built the young couple a small cottage on the fringes of the property. One cold night, while the rest of the family sat around a fire telling stories, Judith held Zeb's hand and pushed out a healthy baby girl named Waynelle Rose. With the assistance of a local midwife, the mother and child recovered peacefully.

Less than a year later in February of 1914, the 78-year-old Emma Biggs was found curled up alone under a large pine tree. James Biggs wrote a letter to family out west inviting them to the funeral. In it, he revealed the circumstances of her passing.

"Her eyes was full opened, and she was smiling like a wolf. Her fingers was bloody all over, like she'd been clawing at something. She was naked as God made her, and huddled up against this old tree on the farm. Larry said there was something in her hand, so we all stood back on account that we figured she'd bite him. He reached down and pried her fingers open. As he bent that last claw over, her mouth dropped open and black vomit come pouring out of her throat and her eyes jumped alive, and she lunged. We all damn near jumped out of our skins thinking she was the devil hisself. She weren't. She fell face down into her own death sick. We found a locket in her hand. Brother Levi's picture was in it. Said it ain't one he gave her, but he gave it to Myrta. Says Emma musta dug it up."

Finally admitting to Myrta's death, ZL Biggs showed them the spot where he'd buried her remains. From a shallow grave, Myrta's body was exhumed by an unknown assailant, and much of her corpse had been consumed. Yet, none of the Biggs would accuse Emma of the deed. ZL insisted, "it most certainly was animals, or the air of death in the casket." Upon the quiet instance of ZL, the bodies were burned and their ashes added to separate urns in the Family Room. Two small framed pictures were scrounged up and placed on the mantel nearby.

Tell-All Account of America's Most Heinous Cannibals

Chapter 5: High On the Hog

ZL Biggs was not a man with whom many trifled, nor was he idle. In 1915, at 79 years old, family pictures showed him as tall and strong as men half his age. And where once the family had struggled to raise 50 head of healthy hogs, Biggs was nearing 1,500 and hungry for more.

"...I do not wish to limit the operation. The problem is that I do not possess the necessary means of production. I met a passionate young man during a visit to London some years ago. Although I did not sympathize with his mad political ideals, he proposed one thing that stood out to me – one must control the means of production. Thus, I have decided to expand the operation tenfold. No longer am I beholden to chintzy railroad yards or greedy butchers. If a job is worth doing, by God, then I will do it."

On February 4, 1916, the *Chattanooga Daily Times* ran an article on the front page proclaiming the evolution of an already burgeoning industry.

"Prosperity Is Within the Grasp of This American Farm...

...Farm to render: Clean and Sanitary! Most Modern Facility to Date. Z. Levi Biggs opens massive new hog processing factory to rival Chicago Stock Yards... New facility is named Biggs Family Farm and Rendering Plant. *Nashville, Chattanooga & St. Louis Railway, owned by Atlantic Coast Line, will build special transfer yard and spur to accommodate increase in freight traffic. At least three hundred fifty additional laborers, butchers, machinists, rail men and stock tenders to begin employment in March. Increase in labor expected as operation expands.*

Biggs often beamed about his successful undertaking, never mentioning specifically who built such a massive facility, or how much it cost. However, he does admit freely who would run the organization.

"My son Zeb will inherit this business soon. Although we will hire many from outside of the family, I have already written letters across the nation to invite all of the Biggs to join and prosper in my labor. Thus far, I have received a warm response from many of my kin who came to the new world after me, including all of my brothers and their children. I believe this is a turning point for the Biggs family."

Indeed, upon building the new Goliath, which worked day and night to topple the Stock Yards in Chicago, Biggs used his influence in Washington to garner lucrative contracts with the US Military. RR Sneed, Tennessee Secretary of State, issued notice to Biggs that on January 1, 1917, the Biggs Family Farm and Rendering Plant would heretofore be known as *Biggs Meats*.

With the new contracts, Biggs Meats, by now the second largest livestock producer in the world, expanded to 350 acres with 2000 separate livestock pens, accommodating 60,000 hogs, 15,000 cattle and 10,000 sheep at any single point in time. What livestock wasn't shipped to Chicago was immediately brought to Biggs Meats, where ZL Biggs cut backroom deals to process for less, giving more back to the farmers, and promising less corruption (but admitting to some!).

Having initially employed only 350 men, the operations immediately expanded to 15,000, some working in hellish conditions day and night. The diary of a Biggs Meats laborer named Joseph D. Connelly reported the all-too-frequent happenings working under such duress.

"This place is a living nightmare... The foremen out here threaten to can us if we complain, and heap more work on our shoulders when we point out machines or lights that ain't working. Day and night, they breathe down our necks making demands and shouting...

"Last week on Saturday, when the sun was down and we couldn't get no lanterns lit on account there was no oil left to burn, fella named Gary Chinsly was trying to open one of the gates that always gets stuck over in 56H. He done opened the latch and crawled up on the gate so he could try to shift his weight and make the thing budge. Well, damnit, he falled down into the pen, and we couldn't even hear him scream over all them damned hogs squealing. He was gone in a few minutes – I mean every part of him and his clothes. It was like the man never existed on God's earth. Ever."

Although concerned citizens and industry organizations raised hackles frequently, and even as the Chicago political machine thrust forth waves of saboteurs, thugs and union agitators, Biggs Meats seemed impermeable. In fact, it was not until WWII that the company unionized its employees, and only then to accommodate another expansion.

Yet, even at his apex, ZL Biggs was unsatisfied. Having grown sleepless and cantankerous, now only taking a breakfast of toast and a single egg each day with no other meals, and apparently subsisting on cold coffee and pipe tobacco throughout his waking hours, Biggs decided to create an even greater legacy. On March 2, 1920, as the roaring twenties began to roll, and as Prohibition had only just begun, Biggs wrote his plans.

"I will send James to Oklahoma to start his life-long desire of starting a carnival and attraction show. My brother Larry has asked to move to Texas to open a chemical factory, so he will write once he finds his location. Georgie is already hard at work in Indiana locating a seam of coal to begin his mining operation; I have sent money and well wishes. My youngest brother, Harry, or as the boys call him, "Popcorn", has always dreamed of making moving pictures since he met Mr. Edison in Chicago. So I have provided him ample account, and he has begun the journey over the Union Pacific Overland route to California where he will begin a career

in pictures. Finally, with some maneuvering, I have assisted Jerry in securing title to a new railroad that shall work with the Biggs family exclusively. He has named it the Illinois, Chattanooga & Pacific Railroad."

One can easily assume ZL Biggs expected to receive all credit in place of his brothers when it came to successful projects. While this was true to some extent, as his brothers were readily willing to heap praise upon their much wealthier, much-respected brother, ZL took a backseat to these affairs. Newspapers rarely described his involvement, and at times, he explained this was agreeable.

"James is not the most honest of men, I must admit. When he built the apparatuses for his carnival games, he revealed to me that each one is rigged in such a way that it is impossible to win without his meddling. I suppose I cannot fault him for taking money from dimwitted rubes in the country. I certainly do not want my name attached to any of his crooked dealing…"

Within a year of leaving, postcards from across the country began to arrive from the brothers. Judith, now the matriarch of the family, and her brother Zeb, carefully read and saved each postcard while tending their many children. One card was received March 24, 1921, from James.

"You all will be pleased to know I've finally taken a wife in my old age. Her name is Patty Suet, but she going to have my name as well, so you can call her Patty Suet-Biggs. She's a younger gal and loves dancing for the boys if they pay. We started a carnival and freakshow out here in Oklahoma we call the Biggs Family Carnival. We have enough kin and friends to open up each night, and we are gaining many more..."

June 27, 1921, a card from Larry asking for funds from ZL to break ground on his chemical plant in Texas. Only months later, having received a small fortune, Larry opened Biggs Chemtrade Refinery, initially creating medical chemicals, drugs, cleaning solvents and shampoos.

Also in June of '21, brother Georgie struck coal and began one of many booming energy interests. The first was named *Allendale Coal Reclamation*. In 1967, upon acquiring a number of smaller competitors, the company was renamed *Sunrise Energy Coal and Oil*. And finally, in late 1979, having capitalized on cheaper oil independent of the Middle East, and having beaten both oil crises, the Biggs family expanded efforts into the *Triad Energy Company*, selling oil to the military, foreign markets, and industrial farm operations — including their own Biggs farm.

By September 7, 1921, brother Jerry's ICP was operational, having pushed out the NC&StL from their yards and carrying hundreds of thousands of fright tons to markets across the south and east between various Biggs interests. Jerry initially acquired a roster of ten steam locomotives, but eventually shifted to three steam locomotives and twenty diesels, this being years ahead of the Southern or Norfolk railways, who primarily relied on steam.

As the line quickly grew, it purchased the *Chattanooga, Lehigh, Chicago & Southern Railway* outright in 1925, followed by the dwindling *Dixie & Cantrell Mine Railway* in 1948 before finally selling to *Norfolk & Western Railway*, the predecessor of *Norfolk Southern*, in 1984.

In its heyday, the ICP Railroad was known as "the Clown Train" by adoring fans across the south because engineers and conductors often donned red clown noses when they saw children. But while the American public appreciated the lighthearted fun it brought kids, Jerry's son Jeremiah, who took control of the line in 1948, complained in a letter to a friend.

"'Nothing but a bunch of clowns' is what I hear every time I'm in New York. I've half a mind to find one of those dirty engineers and slap the damned thing off his face, but Jack, I'm telling you, they hide the sonsofbitches

from me when I'm out in the yards. I make them empty their pockets, their lunchboxes, the toolboxes; I swear to God, there's nowhere to hide the damned things. And yet, every time I'm out somewhere, they say, 'Oh yeah, that funny clown train.'"

Finally, a card arrived on October 12, 1921 from Harry "Popcorn" Biggs, ZL's youngest brother, by now 60 years old. He told of his arrival in California and his hard work finding a film studio. Two years later in 1923, Harry began a B-List operation called *Bucket-O-Laughs Productions*, filming corny slapstick comedy bits with unknown acts. In 1925, at the nudging of his brother James, Harry founded a new company called *Gags 'n' Gaffs Pictures*, filming acrobatic acts, freakshows, circuses, carnivals, and other forms of attraction entertainment, hoping throngs would come see his films rather than the real thing. After its failure, Harry began *Sir Reality Film and Production* in 1931, hoping to attract silent film actors as they departed the industry. As part of the Biggs family push to latch itself onto the US government during the war years, Harry tried filming real war footage to release as newsreel through his *Federal Films* company. Finally, having failed at each venture, and remaining childless with his wife Luanne Dierks-Biggs, Harry opened *Fantast-O-Films* in 1948, focusing on salacious quasi-smut titles, exploitation films and downright gruesome war films such as *I Want the Hobo to Watch*, *Two for Her*, *Black Sheriff*, *Paul's Munnions*, *War Machine* and *The Fuhrer's Hungry Hounds*.

All was well in the Biggs family as they rose ever higher among the rarified atmosphere of American elite. With their patriarch ZL, and with their vast operations sprawling like black tentacles across the country, they absolutely could not falter.

On April 1, 1928, what would have been his 60th wedding anniversary to Emma, a 92- year-old Zebulon Leviathan Biggs woke from only two hours of sleep and went about his chores. His mistress, a young woman named Jennifer Gray who took care of him in the family home, described the events in her journal.

"Daddy woke and went out to the barn for the chickens. He came back to the house with an egg, a small pail of milk and a smudge of butter from the storehouse. He cooked up the egg, had his toast and drank his milk. I was knitting beside him when he turned to me and said, "Jenny, I don't feel well." and I said, "Oh dear, you need to rest. You'll get the cold going out there

in your robe and slippers." And daddy nodded, and I thought he had a little tear in his eyes. Well, he put his hands in his lap, leaned forward and laid his head on the table. He never woke up from it. May God bring some peace to my heart because I haven't stopped crying."

Not only were the Biggs mortified upon his passing, but so were the foundations of the Nation. Many businesses and corporations had lived and died in Biggs' shadow; many fortunes were made, and some lost, with the stroke of his pen. With ZL out of the picture, companies scrambled to figure out next steps, cut backroom deals and attempt to outbid Biggs Meats on future contracts. Over 5,000 attendees packed the floor of the Biggs Meats packing facility, including outgoing US President Calvin Coolidge, both presidential candidates Hoover and Smith, and many heads of companies from across the country, and some from across the world. Even many representatives of the Chicago political machine and the heads of the Stock Yards came to pay respect to a fallen enemy, whom they greatly respected.

After the pomp and circumstance, and after all of the drab ceremony, Judith explained what would become of the fallen patriarch.

"We've placed papa's body in the Family Room near Mama's ashes. Zeb was planning to dump Emma's ashes now that papa was gone, but I said no. Papa always told us to leave her be, and since that's what he would have

wanted, that's what we done. We had Uncle Gus preserve papa real well so he looks just like he's sleeping. It's painful to look over him in that box, but we love him and miss him, and come to see him often yet."

Typically, when such a strong figure passes, a power vacuum ensues, leaving in its wake grisly reminders of how power can corrupt men. However, the Biggs family is not just any family. Resolute and hardened, Judith the mother of five children quietly assumed the duties of the Biggs family. Her brother Zeb took the reins of the company as his father had instructed. Together, they ushered the Biggs family enterprises to their eventual pinnacle.

As the Roaring '20's neared their end, while everyone in the United States believed there were no limits to the riches, the dances, the liquor and the trouble with which they could imbibe, a crack began to race along the surface of the ice. Historical accounts tell of Americans betting on stock markets using credit as well as risky investments. Everyone from shoeshine boys to rich politicians were betting on stocks that couldn't lose. Then, it all broke.

On Tuesday October 29, 1929, known to history as Black Tuesday, after years of sustained wild speculation, the US economy plummeted in a great crash sending markets across the world into a death spiral. That same day, in her little cottage on the fringe of the world's second largest livestock rendering operation, 37-year-old Judith Biggs bore her final child. Albert Herman Webster Biggs.

A printed notice was saved from the windows of the factory.

"The stork just dropped in with a new member of the family! Albert Herman Webster Biggs, weight 7 lbs, arrived October 29, 1929 at 6 in the evening. Factory closed with a day's pay Friday! Come help us celebrate with food, dancing and cold beer! Don't tip off the prohibition agents!"

And what should have been a joyous occasion, in hindsight, was merely the continuation of a horror upon America. Where ZL Biggs had been a shrewd businessman full of moxie, but willing to kill for his own twisted pleasure, Al was the product of inbred parents; hulking, ignorant, and hungry for blood.

Chapter 6: The War Effort

As the country lay paralyzed with economic downturn, Judith Biggs was left to make difficult decisions. Business was consistently dropping, workers were becoming restless thanks to long hours, low wages and and smaller operations in other states were hungry for power. With fewer hogs, cattle and sheep received, Judith writes of her curious decision to diversify profits.

"When we was with mama, I felt at home no matter where we lived. But when mama died, even in papa's arms, I felt like an orphan. I have decided to utilize some of our empty space to take care of those children who lost their homes thanks to this terrible and widespread turn of luck."

On Christmas day 1930, the hastily built *Home for Friendless Children* opened its doors to act as refuge for over 65,000 orphans from 1930 to 1940, many of whom had been shipped into the factory by unscrupulous mayors trying to clear their city streets of young urchins. Unfortunately, there was no statewide accounting for the whereabouts of these children. And although many of the children lovingly referred to

Judith Biggs as "Auntie J", I interviewed someone who claimed to have been taken into the Biggs orphanage. For obvious reasons, I will not use her real name, and instead, we will call her "Amanda". Amanda's account of how the children were treated was typical of any orphanage in that era, however, she explained a curious habit of Auntie J.

"Every Friday, Auntie J and her man Zeb would come into the orphanage walking the floors, looking for kids. They'd come up on one and lead him or her out of the orphanage, and we'd never see them again. They told us these kids were adopted by loving parents, but these "parents" never came into the orphanage."

I was so impressed after interviewing Amanda that I took it upon myself to cast a net to anyone else that had stayed there. One respondent, who we will call

Robert, described a bizarre scene that has left him traumatized until now.

"Us kids knew we were on the premises of a big packing plant, so it was no surprise to hear pigs, cows or lambs screaming all night. But when you hear it every night, you know the difference between a lamb and another kid from the orphanage. First of all, when a lamb screams, it sounds like it's saying, 'Mom!' and that's it. Lambs don't beg for mercy."

While Robert was hesitant to go into additional detail, another resident we'll call Thomas drew out an even more horrific scene.

"There was this door at the end of the building, and this orphanage was huge, right? Like, as big as a factory of its own. Anyways, the door is marked KEEP OUT and was always locked. We was told under no circumstance should any of us kids ever be through that door. Not for nothin', you understand? Nothin'. So of course us boys was always tryin' to sneak a peek in the door, right? Well, one time we got caught, and the fella says, 'It's nothin' but butchered lambs,' and we says, 'So why attach it to the orphanage,' and he says, 'Because - that's why.' Well that's no reason, is it? So one night, I plucked up the courage to go try the door again, and it opened. I went down this hall with all these doors, and in the doors were separate rooms all covered in white tile, and they had these hooks where they would hang the meat. Just like a

packing plant, right? But in the rooms was little kids' blue jeans and pants, shirts, glasses, shoes, right? I mean hats, coats, mittens, the whole thing. They was just piled up in the rooms and covered in blood. So what, you gonna tell me the lambs was walkin' in the place wearin' clothes? Yeah right, buddy."

Interestingly, while livestock numbers were ebbing, meat production stayed the same. One might speculate where the new meat was sourced. From my research, I can say with some degree of confidence that this orphanage had acted as a secondary source for 'special meat' orders to rich clientele. Indeed, a surviving wholesale catalog from this time advertises "Grade-A, Tender Rib Shanks, Cut straight from young lambs" as well as "Young Lamb Liver" and "Economy Grade Shavings from Long Lamb." In any case, as soup lines formed around local churches and businesses to feed the hungry masses, the Biggs Soup Kitchen was praised for its tender vittles.

Larry D. Kirchner of Chattanooga commented in a postcard to family living in Oregon.

"...and I refuse to miss a supper at the Biggs' Soup Kitchen! They have taters and corn and bread, all you can eat. The meat in the stew is the tenderest eating I think I've ever had. I asked one of the men pouring soup what kind of meat he thought it was, and he said it was young calf. He said they had many number of pregnant cows come to slaughter and they get a bonus when she births on the kill floor. I says is there really that many. And he says you better believe it."

At the same time, Judith secured a new twenty-year contract with the United States government to feed dwindling armed forces, utilizing family connections in Washington. While the surface of this arrangement seemed undistinguished to others in the industry, some even commenting publically that Judith would lead the great Biggs business "down into the sewers of hog shit," Judith had foreseen am upcoming conflict, resulting from the downturn in Europe.

As the family business maintained level, there were unforeseen issues with Albert "Al" Biggs at home. After only seven days of school in the fifth grade, Judith received a letter from Al's principal.

"While I certainly appreciate Al's interest in anatomy, I feel uneasy with his 'methods'...

Yesterday, a number of students witnessed Al trap an opossum, tie it to a tree and dissect it alive. I can well appreciate your family's business, but I wonder if it is having an effect on his young mind... I have sent Al home for the day and instructed him to read his books for the evening. I hope you can appreciate how this might upset the younger students. It is admirable for Al to want to take up the family work someday, but until he is of age, I suggest he focuses his attention to his schoolwork, and not on trapping and killing animals on the school yard."

The Biggs: A Family Affair

While the rest of the country nervously watched the conflicts spreading throughout Europe and Asia, Judith and Zeb Biggs hung on with bated breath knowing that their contracts would pay off in spades as soon as war broke with America.

1939, August 31, New York Times.

British Reply to Hitler Narrows the Issue to Free Negotiations with Poland or War; Reich Organizes Defense Cabinet in Crisis.

1940, May 21, New York World-Telegram.

Germans Reach Channel! Million Allies Said To Be 'Isolated'; 'Chute Troops Dropped at the Somme. Reynaud Admits Army 'Disaster'.

1941, December 9, New York Times

U.S. Declares War, Pacific Battle Widens; Manila Area Bombed; 1,500 Dead in Hawaii; Hostile Planes Sighted At San Francisco.

As the United States became deeply entrenched in a two front world war, the Biggs' seemingly ignoble contract to feed the troops grew into a payoff that would be larger than anything else they had ever done, or would ever do. Judith, fast on her feet, quickly acquired four additional packing operations: the *Swift-Hartly Packing* of Missouri, *Kellogg Rendering* in Kansas, *Hotsler Beef and Pork Rendering* in Texas and the *Amends*

Packing Plant in Iowa. With this sudden increase in production, employees now totaled 35,000 men.

During their tours in the Pacific and European theaters, US soldiers often traded their normal rations for the favored "Biggs Meats Packing Co." cans. GIs often commented in letters sent home about the suspiciously good meat.

"Do you remember that stuff we used to feed Charlie [the dog]? The cans had that little Scottie jumping over a ball, and I think it was called Jumping Dog Food? Anyways, I think that's what they're feeding us out here. I'm not complaining – it's actually real good, but I get this sneaking suspicion that it's dog food. But listen, it's so good, I even trade my cigarettes for it, so who's complaining, right?"

Perhaps by no coincidence at all, Biggs Meats formed a subsidiary company named Scrappy Dog Food in an attempt to utilize all consumable scraps from their other operations. One of the advertisements run during the war apologizes for ration shortages –

quite likely the result of the canned food being shipped to US soldiers.

"A Statement to Those Dog Lovers Who Wonder...

As the war goes on, a lot of us wonder more and more just how we're going to feed our dogs. We at Scrappy Dog Foods (who have dogs of our own) would give almost anything to be able to help. Unfortunately, "Scrappy" is rationed by the federal government. The most we dare promise is that customers shall get their fair share of the limited supplies available. Vets, breeders and experts agree that a dog's diet should be balanced in accordance with scientific knowledge. That is why they are in unanimous agreement that Scrappy Dog Foods has solved the dog diet problem. For they know that "Scrappy" is the ideal food for a dog – the complete, scientifically balanced diet that contains just what he needs to keep him perfectly fit. If you are unable to obtain "Scrappy", this at least we can promise: as soon as conditions permit, we shall endeavor to produce enough "Scrappy" to cope with the demand."

Biggs Meats explore d a bevy of methods and products during these critical years of expansion, even as the war ended. Wholesale catalogs advertised products like "CHAM", a sort of Spam knock-off made from various cuts of pork rather than shoulder only; "Royal Loaf", a hideous canned meatloaf made from the same scraps, but including beef and chicken; "Snoob", an animal derived butter replacement similar to margarine; and "Geldo Institutional Gelatin: The Commercial Chef's Treat."

Many of these products lasted only a few years after the war when rationing in America was no longer necessary. Other products, like Spam, were marketed more effectively, and products like Jell-O became the eponymous flag bearers, pushing Geldo out of the marketplace.

The Biggs: A Family Affair

Scrappy Dog Food suffered a different fate, foreshadowing later problems for Biggs Meats. While it was not highly publicized, Scrappy Dog Food stood accused of poisoning over one-thousand dogs, many of which expired after only one serving. While no formal litigation was brought against the company, the Biggs Meats company discretely closed "Scrappy" in 1949.

Chapter 7: Too Big and Failed

Biggs®
Family owned & operated
Quality Meats since 1896!

Whereas most of the Biggs' history to this point was well recorded by journal entries, letters, postcards, photos and newspaper clippings saved by the family, the twenty years between 1941 and 1962 are inexplicably unavailable. In doing additional research outside of the Biggs Archives, I was stunned that the family appears neither in news stories nor in business records. Meanwhile, they were doing a great deal of business processing meat at their five facilities, running machines around the clock.

In 1963, a copy of the *Journal of Business* from the University of Chicago Press included a short article regarding changes in the Biggs family hog operation.

"Biggs Meats, the Tennessee packing behemoth, plans to consolidate operations, closing their Missouri and Kansas divisions and rebrand itself as Biggs Family Rendering. However, don't count this pork producer out as they have recently bid for, and have been awarded, a contract through the U.S. Department of Agriculture to provide pork, chicken and beef to schools across the country."

In this endeavor, the unstoppable moneymaking machine launched what could have been another coup in the livestock processing industry. However, within three months of their first delivery, the company received a concerned letter from a mother in Pennsylvania.

"I would like to share a concern with you about the meat in my son's school lunch. Timothy has never had an allergic reaction to any food, or medicine, in his entire life, so I found it strange when he came home vomiting after eating the meat at school. I asked the principal where they obtained this meat, and they advised me it came from the Department of Agriculture. After an inquiry there, they directed me to you. I would like a full explanation of what is in your meat products that would make my Timothy sick."

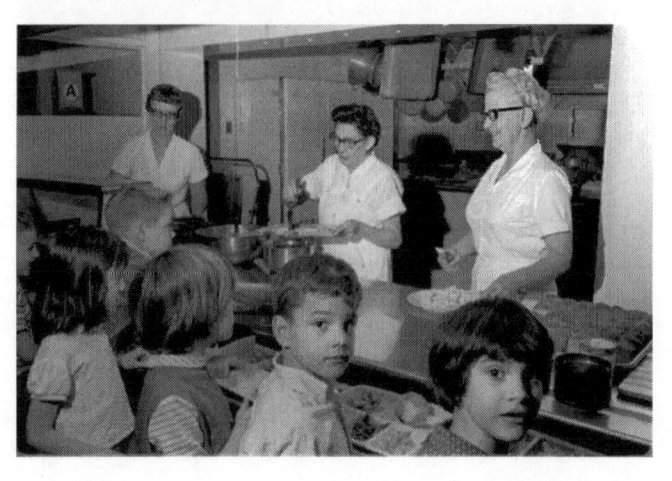

Shortly thereafter, angry letters by the hundred began piling up with the Department of Agriculture demanding information on what was poisoning children across the country. Roughly two years after the first shipments, ten-year-old Dorothy Gillman of Oregon contracted a strange illness after eating her school lunch; chopped ham in beef gravy, macaroni and cheese, and applesauce. Doctors described Dorothy's symptoms as "jerky movements, ataxia and acute memory loss." The girl soon struggled to breathe, and within days, the girl died.

As additional cases were identified, revealing throngs of children experiencing similar symptoms, some of whom died, a task force was formed to investigate the source of infection. Doctors quickly identified the cause to be Variant Creutzfeldt-Jakob disease (vCJD), a form of spongiform encephalopathy, better known as Mad Cow Disease. Authorities immediately began investigating the source of meat, landing on the Biggs Family Rendering plant.

Thus, my law firm became involved in a separate investigation to clear the name of the Biggs family, and to close the books on what they believed to be a "spurious, pointless investigation." However, while years of litigation continued, contracts were no longer offered to the Biggs and their participation in the school lunch program was suspended until the investigation was complete.

Eight years later, as a young law student having only recently joined a firm, I took over this investigation on behalf of the family, researching their case in Judith's cottage where all of her children were born.

Time passed with little headway made in the litigation. The Biggs revealed to my law firm that they were utilizing every political and business contact they had in order that the charges would be dropped. However, inflicted children who survived were winning civil cases each month with no end in sight. The family fortune was taxed mightily, and without additional contracts, straits became dire.

On May 24, 1976, to heap problem upon problem, a distraught 46-year-old Al Biggs scrawled in his diary about more trouble.

"Mama and daddy were out in their Plymouth for a Sunday drive yesterday out in Hixson when they came eastbound on Hamill. A train had already passed through pretty fast, holding daddy at the stop for a minute, and I guess he was in a hurry because he didn't see the other train comin on just as quick. So he run the crossing and there was the accident. The police come out and gave me a card where I could identify mama and daddy's bodies. Honest, I don't think I can do it. They was everything to this family. Everything."

The Biggs: A Family Affair

Like his grandfather ZL Biggs, Al worked with his cousins to taxidermy the remains of Judith and Zeb to be placed in the Family Room. I will confess that I have been in the Biggs Family Room to witness this spectacle. Judith and Zeb's cracked and fractured bodies were reunited with lost limbs, their faces strung back together, hogs teeth replaced many of the lost human teeth and the room resembles some kind of macabre diorama, the couple sitting together on a loveseat holding hands, shiftless, still, staring.

With the loss of his parents, Al Biggs was to take charge of the family business – a now dwindling company that was barely able to break through regular markets other than value processing for small grocery chains. Instead of hammering forward, Al tried to shift gears.

In 1981, a deed of sale reveals that Al purchased a hog farm in Johnston, Iowa, not far from the Amends Packing Plant that the family had previously acquired. By now, control of Amends was wrested back into the hands of the original owning family, and the Biggs were no longer welcome.

On page eight of the June 12, 1981 issue of the Des Moines Register, a short article reveals plans for expansion.

"Albert Biggs, Owner of the Chattanooga, Tennessee packing giant Biggs Family Rendering, plans to team up with Pioneer Hi-Bred in an effort to develop specialized feed corn for livestock.

Biggs, 52, has recently purchased farmland outside of Johnston, near Camp Dodge, in order to house his test hogs. 'We got a pretty square deal from your Lt. Governor Terry Brandstad that allowed us to set up business here,' Biggs explained. 'If all goes well, we hope to open a big packing operation in Iowa; something bigger than Cargill or Swift." Industry insiders say the Biggs operation was harmed during the 1965 of Mad Cow disease that inflicted over 2,000 children nationwide. However, Albert says he is sure business will pick up soon. 'We like Iowa, and we hope Iowa will like us.'"

What was not discussed in the newspaper article, future articles, or even Al's own diary, was that Lt. Governor Brandstad had given Biggs Family Rendering a number of incentives to persuade the family to expand operations into Iowa. The incentives included an almost criminal tax break on both business and personal income, a land grant giving away the acreage in Johnston, and a ten-year deal that would very nearly pay for the entire operation. Just like many previous deals for the Biggs, this one was cut between good old boys, this one taking place in the backrooms of Iowa's gold-domed capitol building.

Back in Chattanooga, the winds were already changing for the other Biggs family businesses. On December 11, 1984, the *Chattanooga Times Free Press* describes the end of a railroading era.

"...after the sudden death of owner Jeremiah Biggs, title to the once-grand Illinois, Chattanooga & Pacific Railroad has passed to family member Louie Dwain "Lefty" Biggs. So too passes an era of the once beloved 'Clown Train' where engineers and conductors once donned red rubber clown noses to entertain children...

Although L.D. Biggs says he enjoyed the noses, he admits the change is necessary. 'We're currently promoting Operation Lifesaver, which is a nationwide effort to 'Look Listen Live' and thereby reduce railroad accidents across the country. We used to have fun with the clown noses, but too many folks were approaching fast moving trains to get pictures."

Less than two years later, on January 4, 1986, while the railroad continued to reorganize and abandon trackage throughout the south, the Interstate Commerce Commission approved a merger of the ICP with its much larger competitor *Norfolk & Western*, effective July 1, 1986. Almost all rolling stock and diesel engines were sold, and no stock remains to evidence the once- profitable road.

By 1990, as many of the Biggs family enterprises had either been sold or closed, Al Biggs made a final attempt to bring the ailing Biggs Family Rendering back from the brink. However, the Chicago Tribune described, not without a little satisfaction, the results of the effort.

"Hormel Foods Corporation has beat out Biggs Family Rendering in a bid to provide MREs (Meals Ready to Eat) for US soldiers fighting in the Gulf. With the loss of the deal, the once giant Biggs company is facing certain bankruptcy as it fails to sell its products across the country."

Stark writing was on the Biggs family wall. Without a major contract, and without any channels to distribute goods, Biggs Family Rendering had nearly zero outlets in a market dominated by giant agri-processors, who produced clean, edible products. Ninety-seven years after their founding patriarch began his dream of operating a massive butchering operation in Chattanooga, *The New York Times* unceremoniously described the end of the Biggs Family Rendering company in a small article mixed among the back pages.

"The Biggs Family Rendering company is liquidating in the face of recent bankruptcy filings. The owner of the plant, Albert Biggs, shuttered the ailing factory on August 1, 1993 with plans to sell all assets by the end of this year. The company entered bankruptcy negotiations after a failed bid for US government contracts, as well as an investigation into a 1965 outbreak of Mad Cow disease in humans."

I interviewed Al Biggs after the sale of the properties shortly before he ceded title of his family home.

> *"We plan to move to Iowa where I still got a hog farm operation, although it's really small compared to grandad's yards. I mean I really hate to leave here because this is where our family growed up and prospered for a hundred years. I feel like I let down the whole family. But we have to keep tryin' so we gonna raise hogs on a 'heritage' farm and just make ends meet."*

By early 1994, Al Biggs, his wife Loretta and his two children moved to the farm in Iowa, never to see their ancestral home again.

As bodies continued to be snatched, as children continued to vanish and as hogs grew fatter, the only change in the pattern seemed to move victims from Tennessee to Iowa. Meanwhile, Al Biggs had grown distant from his family, and distant from the hog farming business, often letting his wife and children manage affairs without him.

During the summer of 1995, Al invited his "brother" Trig Biggs to Iowa to stay with the family. It's worth mention that I can find factual relation between Al and Trig. However, Trig has confided that Judith and Zeb had one more child, unrecorded, and left him in the care of another Biggs relative. While no one can confirm this assertion, for purposes of this story, we shall assume Trig is somehow related.

With the assistance of Trig on the family farm, and now entering his eighties, Al Biggs had become restless like his grandfather, deciding to branch out of the farming business. The Des Moines Register reported this new affair in October 2010.

"In what some might say was a strange form of preservation, local amateur Albert Biggs says he has created what may be the world's first and only seasonal museum. The Slaughter House plans to exhibit Biggs' version of livestock raising, rendering and production, which will also include farm animal oddities... Biggs claims that tour guides will be dressed as 'butchers' as customers walk you through the exhibits...He hopes the Halloween seasons brings many out to his 'Slaughter House'."

Much like his grandfather's exhibit at the Chicago World's Fair, Al Biggs' bizarre museum display saw modest turnout in the Des Moines, Iowa metro. However, having somehow grossly miscalculated his approach, Al was mortified when customers ran from the attraction screaming. Where he had bet on customers enjoying a lesson in farm husbandry, what he found was that a cult following grew, claiming his museum was a so-called "haunted attraction".

Depressed and exhausted, Biggs immediately sold the attraction to his brother Trig who agreed to take care of the "living museum" in honor of their grandfather. Trig subsequently renamed it *The*

Slaughterhouse, moving it outside of the Des Moines city limits, and away from prying eyes of investigators looking for the bodies of at least two dozen customers that had never returned.

Chapter 8: A Haunting Future

As Al became ever more reclusive at the family farm, only interested in raising hybrid livestock, and still obsessing over development of a "perfect" genetically modified corn, his brother Trig put the word out to the rest of the Biggs family across the country.

"I told 'em all to come on down, help out with Al's farm, you know...help me out at The Slaughterhouse where we tag 'em and bag 'em, bang 'em and hang 'em, scare 'em and tear 'em. It's a real fine enterprise, this haunted thing. See, we're working during the off-season raisin' hogs and killin' 'em for food and profit. But out here, after all the family business has been taken care of for the year, we love showin' little piggies just how we do it."

After hard luck hopping trains and looking for work, Lefty Biggs moved to Iowa to help his kin Trig in operating the events. Many more family arrived by bus, car, airplane and passenger train, each with an agenda for blood.

Little time passed before authorities began sniffing around the Biggs' Pleasant Hill location where, night after night, customers to their "haunted attraction" went missing, sometimes ending up as part of the spectacle, other times ending up in the food. Reports flooded in about lost children, lost husbands and wives, and even lost pets. Trig maintained his stance on patrons.

"How is it I'm responsible for what everyone's kids is up to? I don't know where these little rats end up at the end of the night. I ain't in charge o'keepin them on a leash and makin sure they get back home to mommy and daddy safe. Man, that's what school is for. And books. Why ain't these kids readin books? Cause they wanna have fun is why. But that ain't my problem. I give 'em the fun and they come out here to have a good time. So what if they never come home. Go out to Toys R Us and bitch about it to that big Gorilla named Georgie, or whatever it is they got out there, what who's tellin them kids to never grow up. You gotta problem with fun, go out there and rattle that idiot's cage. Don't come here gettin all bent up on me. No sir."

Meanwhile, the hogs on the family farm were growing fatter and hungrier for human blood.

The disappearances finally grew intolerable, and the Biggs boys had to close their living museum and go into hiding in 2014. However, it wasn't long before the old family connections were struck once more, and federal investigators were called off.

In November 2016, after securing a large grant from the United States government, Trig and Lefty Biggs moved operations to a new location in Des Moines, Iowa. Striking a deal with the living relatives of PT Barnum, the Biggs duo opened in the former Iowa Paint Factory, claiming to be a "new and improved Slaughterhouse."

Although I have never visited this Slaughterhouse museum, I have seen the bizarre building plans on public record, which include ample soundproofing, seemingly unnecessary grease traps, hundreds of strange machines with no reported purpose, blood drainage and massive sewer hookups.

In October 2017, the haunted attraction opened its doors once more to unsuspecting customers claiming it would be the "scariest" experience of the season. However, in a tearful interview, one customer named Kelly Whitfield claims it was much more than scary.

"My friend Susan and I went with our friends for Halloween because we'd heard so much about it on Facebook. It started ok, it was kinda scary, but it was just a haunted house, you know? But then they made us get on these carts in the dark, and we had to ride down a long hall in pitch black. When we got off the carts, Susan wasn't there anymore. We never found her. We called

the police, called her parents, everything. And we never saw her again."

Another account from a terrified spouse explains how she was waiting for her husband after the show.

"They separated us for some reason, and made us sit on different cart. I lost Sam back there in the dark. We...we just got married two months ago, and we were so excited to meet our friends as this newlywed couple, you know? And then...and then he was gone. I thought I heard him scream somewhere, but all I could do was move forward...they just kept pushing us forward. And he was in there, somewhere, screaming. Screaming. And I never saw him again."

Hundreds more of these accounts go on to describe dark halls filled with stench, an arm grabbing a friend from the darkness, lost love ones, missing children, and silence. It is the silence which terrifies me and which should terrify you. For it is not the 'fun' of Halloween that should scare you, or even going to so-called haunted houses; what should scare every reader is the insidious, evil, ever-watching, ever-hungry Biggs family who uses their operation as a front for kidnapping, murder and cannibalization.

What will you do as you walk through the front doors, stand in line and present your ticket? Will you run? Many have tried only to be dragged back in by some rough handed monster butcher. Oh sure, it's for fun. Always for fun. But what will happen when you are shoved onto their steel carts and dragged into the black bowels of their factory? Will your mouth be sewn shut just like 16-year-old Susan Philmore's was before she escaped and ran away, only to be discredited by the police? Will your family ever realize that your body was hung, sliced and devoured by a family of cannibals in their 'haunted house'? Likely not.

I contacted Trig and Lefty Biggs on a conference call one last time prior to completing this historical account. I asked Trig what was in store for customers in coming years after their grand reopening. As expected, he promised fun, excitement and terror for all of his "little piggies" coming through. He even sent me excruciating pictures of dismembered bodies, which he claimed were "new props" for upcoming "tours".

Perhaps in an effort to force a confession from the two butchers, I asked Lefty what would happen to all of those children who disappeared in the darkness of his haunted house. He left me with a single phrase before disconnecting the call.

"Just you wait…"

Made in the USA
Middletown, DE
17 September 2024